DESIGNERS ABROAD

MICHELE KEITH

DESIGNERS ABROAD

INSIDE THE VACATION HOMES OF TOP DECORATORS

THE MONACELLI PRESS

To my parents—for instilling in me a love of travel and
a curiosity about the world.

All rights reserved. Published in the United States
by The Monacelli Press, LLC, New York.

Library of Congress
Cataloging-in-Publication Data

Keith, Michele.
Designers abroad: inside the vacation homes of top
decorators/Michele Keith.
pages cm
ISBN 978-1-58093-351-3 (hardback)
1. Interior decorators—Homes and haunts. 2. Interior
decoration. 3. Vacation homes.
I. Title.
NK2115.3.I57K448 2013
747—dc23   2012040182

www.monacellipress.com

Printed in China

Designed by Michelle Leong

CONTENTS

PREFACE

I remember my first trip outside the United States so well, flying to Cuba with my two sisters and parents, exploring every nook and cranny of Havana, and driving from one end of the island to the other, stopping whenever something of interest popped up. It was prior to the Revolution, and while I was only six, the graceful architecture, delicious food, sandy beaches, and friendly people made a huge impression on me.

Perhaps that's why I've been an inveterate traveler ever since. As a sometime *flâneuse*, I've often wondered what kinds of rooms might exist behind the walls I could often only experience from the outside. And so the idea to write a book about overseas interiors took shape. Coupled with the many gifted contacts I've made in the interior design industry over the years, the idea gradually became a reality as designers graciously offered me images of their own homes abroad. I find it fascinating to learn about how each worked within the physical vocabulary of different cultures and dealt with their inherent challenges—monsoons, locations that delivery-men could only access by boat or mule, and contractors who perhaps work at a more leisurely pace than we are used to, to name a few. As the project developed, I became most interested in seeing to what extent the interiors reflected the host countries, and how designers interwove their own personalities with traditional furnishings. It was fun to see to what extent decorators "went native," concocted a personalized mix of things from all over the globe, or replicated their stateside abodes to some degree. More than a few projects took me completely by surprise. It seems a yen for adventure and appreciation of the talents of local craftsmen are as deeply embedded in these designers' DNA as an understanding of color and proportion.

I hope you find the book a source of inspiration for infusing a bit of the exotic into your own home's décor, or for incorporating objects from vacation travels into its rooms, and that you enjoy taking this round-the-world journey as much as I did.

—Michele Keith

TROPICAL ESCAPES

cortney and robert novogratz
TRANCOSO, BRAZIL

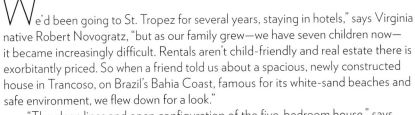

"We'd been going to St. Tropez for several years, staying in hotels," says Virginia native Robert Novogratz, "but as our family grew—we have seven children now—it became increasingly difficult. Rentals aren't child-friendly and real estate there is exorbitantly priced. So when a friend told us about a spacious, newly constructed house in Trancoso, on Brazil's Bahia Coast, famous for its white-sand beaches and safe environment, we flew down for a look."

"The clean lines and open configuration of the five-bedroom house," says Cortney, his wife and design partner, "are more 'us' than the majority of typically folk-art homes there." It also suits the couple's affinity for mixing high- and low-end, vintage and modern pieces against a neutral backdrop. Set on a hilltop just minutes from the beach, the house's elevation provides both a spectacular panorama and dry breezes that make salty ocean air, which can play havoc with decorating, a nonissue.

The indoor-outdoor feeling is established first by a 10-foot-wide wraparound porch, polished cement floors, and a color scheme that showcases the diverse Brazilian woods used for the furnishings. Comfortable and low-maintenance, it projects the sensibility of a boutique hotel, the couple says, and with a swimming pool, outdoor bar, pool table, mini soccer field, and tree house, it certainly has all the same amenities.

"Doing the place was such fun because there are so many talented local craftsmen," Robert says. "Just look at the 2-foot-square hanging light fixtures made by Fábio Santos of *piaçava* fiber." Artisans also produced most of the big pieces from sketches made by the designers, such as the salvaged *angelim* dining table and *tatajuba* bathroom vanities. As for accessories and accent pieces—both for themselves and clients back home—the entire family piles into their "hippie" van and visits the flea markets of Belo Horizonte. Several 1940s and 1950s pieces were found on one outing. The family also keeps tabs on the street vendors in Porto Seguro, where they have ferreted out such beauties as the antique chair in one of the guest bedrooms.

With three-hundred-and-sixty-degree views, only a few pops of color are necessary to make the décor feel complete, so the couple supplied them with art. The Union Jack by Ann Carrington, pieced together with denim and plaid fabric, "adds a world-traveler vibe to the house," says Cortney; a green-and-white button portrait of Robert's favorite tennis star, Björn Borg, is also by the same artist. Painted skateboards imaginatively turned into "art" jazz up the bar.

A home is much better than a hotel, they say. "All the toys—golf clubs, tennis racquets, dune buggy—are here. We come for August, and sometimes for two weeks in March, a few clothes and books in hand, and immediately we're in relaxation mode."

LEFT *Designed as a loft with a Brazilian beat, the ground floor stretches from a conversation area—furnished with a wooden bench purchased from a bar going out of business—to a kitchen-and-dining-room that features a 14-foot-long table of salvaged wood designed by the couple.* **PREVIOUS PAGES, RIGHT** *Twig-shaded lamps and fresh flowers make a bar near the pool a favorite family hangout.*

RIGHT *"Big walls call for big art,"
Robert Novogratz says, and puts
theory into practice with a Union Jack
collage assembled by Ann Carrington
in the living room. Washable denim
cushions on handmade wood benches
and a polished cement floor make
for easy housekeeping.* **OVERLEAF**
*Created from linen and twigs, the
porch lights were designed by Robert
to complement the oar-like trimmed
ceiling. Shaded clerestory windows
increase light penetration to the interior
while keeping direct sunlight out.
The sliding doors, however, are nearly
always left open to take advantage
of the sea breezes.*

BELOW *A pergola creates a perfect spot for relaxing between dips in the pool or catching up on reading. With sandy feet–friendly cushioned benches and a vine-covered roof, it's used day and night by family and guests.*

RIGHT *One of the couple's twin boys perches on a lacquered coffee table. Roll-up, matchstick twig shades keep light to a minimum as locally woven fabric spreads cheer the space.*

diane burn
SAN PEDRO, TABOGA ISLAND, PANAMA

Panama's Taboga Island has *almost* cured my chronic wanderlust," says Diane Burn, who has lived in San Francisco, New York, Palm Beach, Porto Ercole, and Paris. This "Island of Flowers" lies twelve miles south of Panama City and has changed little over many decades. The area is so geared toward vacationers, however, that the designer had difficulty finding the basics she needed to renovate her "little shack," as she calls it. "I couldn't find anything I needed, even nails or sandpaper."

Mesmerized by the location high on a hill overlooking the sixteenth-century town of San Pedro and views of the mainland, Burn took on the challenge. To begin, she rounded up a "dream team" of collaborators: local craftsman-builder Armando Lopez, who did everything from constructing exterior walls to building cement banquettes; New York trompe l'œil artist Karin Linder, who turned the cement floors into ancient "stone" and painted walls, faux pediments, and moldings that suggest another century, and Miami-based garden designer Tony Urrutia, who developed the grounds and served as translator. Burn purchased a penthouse in the capital during construction to serve as a design studio and to store furnishings as she gathered them.

Gutting the house, installing a tin roof five feet higher than the original, adding a second wing, and making armoires out of old doors meant a lot of intensive labor, and the location meant that much of it had to be done almost completely by hand. Burn believes that "Doing things the old-fashioned way gives a house a rich patina that can't be obtained otherwise."

Although she's known professionally for gentle color palettes, Burn took the opposite direction here. Referring to the jungle of mango, lime, lemon, and papaya trees behind the house, she says, "I felt the environment and local culture demanded vivid shades, and knew using them would produce a visual flow from the outside in. It was an interesting experience, and opened my eyes to a scope of new possibilities." Her bedroom, however, a cloud of white, coral, and verdigris, is done in soft, romantic hues, "shades in which anyone would feel relaxed and inspired." Burn scouted fabrics in neighboring countries, imported plumbing fixtures from the U.S., and found the decorative ironwork that Lopez fashioned into a fan window for the kitchen at Matildo's Art, Antiques & Furniture in Panama City.

Not one to sit still for very long, Burn is thinking of ways to continue improving the property. "I've always dreamt of having a boutique hotel," she confesses. Casa La Choza, or "The Shack-House," is certainly a cleverly tongue-in-cheek, self-deprecating name for one so well appointed.

LEFT *The living room's daybed is layered with Guatemalan ouipils; the ceramic wall plaques originated in Nove, Italy; and the stacked wooden trays, although purchased in Panama City, are Indian. An Italian iron candelabrum* *embellishes a corner and helps to establish a motif of that material throughout the house.* **BELOW** *A fan painted to look rusty whirls above an Indian dining table. The top half of a buffet displays Colombian artifacts.*

BELOW The terrace, pretty as a picture with a view to El Morro Island in the distance, is encircled with a railing, circa 1800, from a house in Casco Viejo, Panama City's historic district. The chairs, replicated from French originals, were made by a local craftsman. **RIGHT** A Louis XVI baldachin has accompanied Burn on every move, and again sets the tone for her bedroom in Panama. A decorative Italian plaster relief hangs on the wall below it; the table lamps have iron bases and parchment shades faux-finished to replicate its verdigris color.

michael la rocca and jack kelly
GALLE, SRI LANKA

The trip getting here is definitely crazy," says New York-based Michael La Rocca, "twenty-four hours! But I can't imagine not having our Sri Lanka house." How did he end up on the island nation? "My partner, Jack Kelly, a design consultant, was trekking in Nepal when the royal family was assassinated. He had to leave immediately, not knowing what kind of turmoil might ensue. The only plane taking off anytime soon was headed for Colombo, so he took it."

Kelly used the unexpected time on the island to travel around. Intrigued by his glowing reports, La Rocca joined him and agreed that the white-sand beaches, fresh fish from the sea, and interesting people constituted a mini-paradise. The two immediately began thinking about building and soon located the perfect spot, in Galle, on the Indian Ocean. Making the land purchase took a "leap of faith," since they were unfamiliar with local customs and laws, but they pressed forward.

The starting point for their design was a photograph of a 1920s home on a Pacific island that Kelly had found. The pair began sketching, combining elements of that structure with Colonial influences and Palladian nuances. The result is an open, airy house that honors the tropical locale.

Eight months later, construction of the single-level, 6,000-square-foot dwelling began. While Sri Lanka is extremely hot, the house's design keeps the interior feeling cool. The symmetrical retreat features gleaming hardwood and stained-and-scored concrete floors that welcome bare feet, stark white plaster-over-concrete walls, ceiling fans to create gentle breezes, and trellised woodwork on everything from cupboards to doors to ensure airflow. "I stay five to six weeks a year," says La Rocca, "and Jack goes back and forth regularly, so comfort equals aesthetics in importance, ergo, we do have air-conditioned bedrooms."

As to the furnishings, "Sri Lankan craftsmen are very versatile," says Kelly. "We draw what we want—bed, table, armoire—and they make it. The quality is good, and because pieces are handcrafted they have a special, very personalized veneer." Local talent also made the living room's graceful metal chandelier after a prototype La Rocca designed and the giant, polished-cement nautilus shells fashioned by Kelly, from which water streams into the glass-tiled, sunken bathtubs. They also give local fine artists photographs or sketched ideas for a theme, or even just a guideline for colors. Pieces are usually finished within days.

Furnishings are purposefully eclectic and international. The living room's 1930s Jaffna chairs were purchased in a store in Colombo, and the painted-wood statues guarding the front door are from India. The shell-encrusted table topped with marble dividing the living room into two conversation areas, though, they made themselves. "We must have spent a whole week picking up shells on the beach," Kelly recalls with a laugh.

"The country has changed radically over the past twelve years—it's much more European now," says La Rocca. "But there's still a laissez-faire culture. We relax, tour around, swim, and give lots of dinner parties. It's the antithesis of New York."

LEFT *Aged mahogany found in an abandoned tea-storage building helps the bed it eventually became meld with older furnishings from the 1930s and 1940s. The designers commissioned the coral painting from a* local artist. **BELOW** *Sapphires, rubies, and black onyx sparkle on the raiment of a Krishna Raja Wadiyar IV portrait from India. The nineteenth-century table beneath was purchased in Hong Kong. The furniture is painted rattan.* **PREVIOUS PAGES** *Capturing the essence of Colonial comfort, a living room with 40-foot-high ceilings glows with buffed hardwood floors, offers ample seating, and contains a heady mixture of art and sculptures.*

BELOW *The master bath—identical to the guest room's—features a sunken tub and a mahogany vanity and doors. The floor is polished, stained, and scored concrete.* **RIGHT** *South African cowhide upholsters Jaffna chairs.*

To the designers' surprise, the intense humidity causes their brass lamps to tarnish quickly, but they learned to love the look. The painting of a punkah wallah was purchased at an Indian auction.

andrew fisher and jeffry weisman
SAN MIGUEL DE ALLENDE, MEXICO

We always imagined owning a beach house in a foreign country," says Jeffry Weisman, "and looked every time we vacationed in Mexico." "But nothing spoke to us until, ironically, we visited hillside San Miguel de Allende, which was founded in the sixteenth century," continues Andrew Fisher. "It's a UNESCO World Heritage site that overflows with Colonial charm. Add the expat community and talented artisans, and we couldn't ask for better."

They found a house with an unusual L-shaped plan—as opposed to the traditional Mexican layout surrounding a courtyard—that guarantees cross-ventilation and views from every room, but its "staggeringly beautiful" garden lush with flowering jacaranda trees sealed the deal. They both agreed that work was needed on the interior. "We became captivated with the creativity of the contractor and the skills of the craftsmen," Weisman says, "so we decided to gut the original 5,500 square feet and add 1,500 more. It was the easiest project we've ever done. We had nothing but fun and finished in a record-breaking six months."

Driving the design was the feel for an authentic Mexico they had developed over the years, along with a love of blue and white. About half of the furnishings were purchased or made locally. A few signature pieces, like the dining room's mother-of-pearl, seashell, and green glass chandelier, and a clever breakfast-room armoire whose mirror is actually a door to Fisher's studio, crept in.

Ebullient hosts who like nothing better than giving dinners for twenty-four, the two always welcome guests—when the four spare rooms are full they bunk on fireside chaise longues that convert into beds. The pair has also amassed a rich variety of items from around the globe and use many here, particularly in the guest rooms. "When we travel, we shop," explains Weisman with a grin. Antique painted panels that once decorated the ceiling of a Japanese temple, a chair of their own creation crafted in San Francisco, and a chest inlaid with camel bone picked up in India come from disparate regions, but, arranged as they are, produce a feeling of a new Mexico. A gleaming, herringbone-patterned, terra-cotta floor, antiqued by a laborious process involving a compound of tar and gasoline, forms the perfect neutral backdrop to the varied collection. The master bedroom holds a completely different mix: an antique Moroccan rug found at Insh'ala, a local store; a 1930s French settee upholstered in silk-velvet ikat bought in Istanbul; and bedside lamps from Hearst Castle. This mélange of pieces from different provenances informs the entire house, including the kitchen, where cupboards of antique, weathered pine beams glow beneath a Belle Epoque chandelier and a high frieze of blue-and-white tiles made in nearby Dolores Hidalgo, from a design painted by Fisher.

"We weren't planning to work here," says Weisman. "It just happened." Now they're in residence half the year. And while relaxing is not their specialty, they find they adjust easily to the slower pace soon after they arrive. "Spending so much time working remotely from our San Francisco office and having the quiet and space makes everything feel like a vacation. It's really changed our lives," he says.

LEFT *Fisher's artistic composition of gold leaf, paint, and fragments of reclaimed plastic tarp conceals a television above a fireplace carved of local cantera stone. The pint-sized, eighteenth-century Spanish chairs* *retain their original, embossed leather seats and backs.* **BELOW** *Fisher, an avid cook, designed the kitchen as well as the mesquite table—and forged its legs from bronze.* **PREVIOUS PAGE** *The master bedroom's alder-wood* *desk decorated with cast bronze stars is a Fisher Weisman design custom built to conceal an air conditioner. The Queen Anne chair—referred to in the household as "Andrew's bed of nails"— is encrusted with seashells.*

LEFT *Fisher's collage of painted and quilted coffee filters reigns over a living room framed on either side by a pair of James Mont's carved-wood lamps, circa 1940. Upholstered in woven peacock feathers, a quartet of ottomans provide extra seating or serve as side tables when topped with laurelwood trays. Layered antique Moroccan rugs add texture to the floor.* **PREVIOUS PAGES** *An ornate chandelier conceived by Fisher and executed by Weisman is anchored by the presence of a large round walnut table and set of chairs. To either side of a midcentury mirror discovered in Mexico City are candelabra Fisher crafted from andirons and embellished with faux coral and crystal beads.*

The master bedroom is filled with Fisher's 24-karat-splashed artwork and fitted with a chair, ottoman, and headboard upholstered in velvet and trimmed with yardage cut from fifty-year-old batik skirts bought in Chiang Mai, Thailand.

LEFT *A substantial four-poster bed and wood cabinet crafted locally anchor a guest room curtained in silk-and-cotton ikat. A zigzag pattern adds unexpected texture to a recent ceiling renovation.*

BELOW *Fisher's work of linen, paper, and pushpins coated in gesso and 24-karat gold counters an eighteenth-century stone wall, endowing a study with a unique contrast in textures.*

Silk-velvet ikat from Istanbul covers a French wing chair poised next to a gilded-bronze gueridon—both date to nineteenth-century France.

trisha wilson
VAALWATER, SOUTH AFRICA

This country speaks to my soul," says Trisha Wilson of Vaalwater, located within the Welgevonden Game Reserve in Limpopo, South Africa. "It feels like home—Texas— the openness, weather, and warmth of the people."

Introduced to the area in the 1990s while working on a project for a local hotelier, the designer immediately fell in love with the landscape and began seeking out a place of her own. A site in the heart of the reserve started as a house for herself, grew into a compound for visiting friends, and then became a guest retreat. "The quintessential African landscape, Waterberg Mountains, variety of game, it took my breath away," she says. "It still does."

She aimed to create a traditional but elegant bush camp integrated into the topography with her design. Framed views, native stone plinths, sand-colored hand-plastered walls, natural gum poles, and thatched roofs help the lodge she calls "Izingwe"—Zulu for leopard, a symbol of wisdom among some tribes—blend well with the surroundings. "It's my home away from home for three or four weeks at least twice a year," she says, "where I regain my balance and get energized."

To strengthen the lodge's contextual roots, Wilson sought out African artists to craft woven-grass floor coverings, furniture, and artwork such as the animal-emblazoned columns on the veranda, by Gift Chiseko. "You can find wonderful sculptors working in wood and stone nearby, or any number of beautiful objects at Black Mamba Art and Crafts Gallery. I also love the Zulu telephone-wire baskets decorating the bar's back wall," she says. An easy, low-key mood infiltrates each room; endless views of the savannah create a borderless sense of place. The main building includes living and dining areas, a terrace, and bar; the dining room features a floor of stained concrete with a pebble-design inset; and the welcoming lounge offers a huge, zebra-upholstered ottoman, overstuffed sofas, and gently glowing chandelier. "I think of design as telling a story about the person who inhabits the space," she says. Many of the accessories, such as the entrance hall's palm-sized "passport" masks used long ago by different tribes, for example, come from her own travels.

The bedroom in Wilson's private 855-square-foot villa is based on a scheme of textures and handcrafts, creating a comfortably authentic space. It's clever, too— a refrigerator, bar, and storage area are hidden behind panelized photographs. The bath is tranquil; the outdoor panorama is all the decoration needed. A eucalyptus-floored balcony extends into a *sala*, or thatched-roof pavilion. "It's a wonderful perch for spying on the animals," she says, "or to watch the sun go down with a hint of light twinkling from the bead-and-porcupine-quill chandelier."

"Yes, we had plenty of problems constructing Izingwe," recalls Wilson, remembering torrential rains; how the sandy terrain made truck passage impossible so that cows had to transport sofas, lamps, and mirrors on their backs; and discovering she needed a fence to keep the lions out. "It was all worth it. I never tire of being here."

RIGHT *Bar furniture made of gum-wood—a type of eucalyptus—and a fireplace decorated with native rocks unearthed during construction help to endow the room with a sense of place. The rug was sourced at a roadside market.* **BELOW** *Lined with varnished gum-wood poles, the bar's walls are also decorated with an assortment of indigenous masks, drums, spears, beaded baskets, art, and wire bowls.* **PREVIOUS PAGES** *In the traditional African bush camp tradition, the living room features a thatched roof and hand-plastered walls. Anchored with a woven-grass rug, a cozy conversation area is lit by a chandelier representing monkeys holding alabaster ostrich eggs that was designed by Wilson and crafted by local artisans.*

LEFT *The dining room's mahogany table and needlepoint-cushioned walnut chairs are local finds, while the Colonial-era silver candelabrum hails from London's Portobello Road. The fireplace screen represents lizards and dragonflies, prevalent in the region.*
BELOW *Tribal masks Wilson found while traveling around the country decorate the veranda's coffee table, which is made of recycled railway ties.*

RIGHT *Wilson's spacious bedroom, carpeted in woven-grass matting, continues the bush theme in elegant fashion with a four-poster mahogany bed reminiscent of an antelope's horns, topped with eagles. A zebra-striped bench and cane chair complete the décor.* **OVERLEAF** *Zebra-skin pillows enliven rattan furniture on the veranda. Its main focal point, a large leadwood tree trunk, depicts baboons, elephants, wildebeest, and other safari animals and was carved by Zimbabwean artist Gift Chiseko with hand tools and a chain saw.*

inson dubois wood
LAMPHUN, THAILAND

Shuttling around the world comes easily to Inson Dubois Wood. Born in Connecticut to a French mother and Thai father, he summered and wintered alternately in Europe and Asia as a child, but has called New York City home for most of his adult life. So when he inherited a 100-acre property in Lamphun, Thailand, from his grandfather, he immediately had the idea of building a vacation residence, complete with guest cottages.

The town is twenty miles south of tourist-thronged Chiang Mai, in a rural area inhabited primarily by farmers—many of whom are also fine artists and craftsmen—and where street life centers on vendors selling exotic fruits, birds to buy and set free to symbolize the Buddhist concept of nonattachment, and flowers and incense for temple offerings. It took about a decade for Wood to finish his "European-bohemian-contemporary-Thai-styled Zen retreat," as he portrays it. Clients kept him busy at home and Thailand's monsoon seasons would stall progress for weeks on end. He did not have an urgent need for a getaway place and he was happy to allow the "extremely talented team of local craftspeople who take great pride in their skills" to work in a way that was comfortable to them. The slow pace was acceptable and, in fact, provided him with ample time to design the majority of the furniture, which was fabricated on site.

An atmosphere of peacefulness and harmony encompasses his 6,000-square-foot aerie, possibly due to the hand construction. "You can almost sense that no electric sawing occurred," Wood says. The emphasis on ceramic, stone, and solid teak—some reclaimed from 200-year-old rice barns—adds to the feeling. Subtle contrasts encourage a closer look at practically every object. Sit-up-straight chairs surrounding a breakfast table display the designer's carved interpretation of ancient dragons while smooth, gently rounded wood pieces populate an open-format living room; a twentieth-century mirror created with an undulating wood centerpiece from Africa decorates the granite river stone fireplace chimney, playing off the strict lines of the classical Thai chair from the 1860s close by.

In addition to the public quarters, the house comprises five bedrooms—with beds draped in silk from Shinawatra, a store known for its first-rate selection of antique and new fabrics—a gallery/studio Wood uses to paint, sculpt, and showcase art, the majority of it indigenous to the province; an extensive porch encircling most of the house, fitted with fire pits for impromptu barbecues and lounge chairs for reading and snoozing; and an enormous white party space. He points out, "It's considered impolite not to entertain all your neighbors at least once during the year." In between gala dinner parties, planning future projects, and occasional bike rides into the countryside, Wood can be found floating serenely in the pool that looks for all the world like a lotus pond.

LEFT *A custom, 20-foot-long teak table with matching stools is set with antique ceramic dishes from Japan and Thai terra-cotta vessels. The gourd-shaped sculpture is by a local artist.* *A san phra phum, or spirit house, stands beyond in the garden.* **BELOW** *Examples of Wood's vast collection of sensual teak sculptures made by local artists.* **OVERLEAF** *A 2,000-year-old,* *cast-bronze Buddha receives deferential placement on a pyramid of small tables. The wood carving above the statuette was created by a local farmer.*

LEFT *Used strictly for parties, an open white space is designed with modern metal joists and purlins, and is centered with a floor-to-ceiling concrete fountain.*

BELOW *Six-foot-long sculptures carved from reclaimed tree stumps by a local artist are a favorite of Wood's.*

BELOW *The guest room walls, designed with ample cupboards, are made of woven bamboo, as is the ceiling, and trimmed with teak. An abstract interpretation of the four* *seasons is represented in the woodcut above a bed dressed in silk from Shinawatra.* **RIGHT** *Christopher Hyland bed linens are accented with a traditional rectangular pillow covered* *in antique silk. Sculptures of African soapstone adorn the side tables, and a Thai folding pillow embellished with mudmee silk, the northern Thai version of ikat, rests at the bed's foot.*

SIMPLE
SANCTUARIES

lucien rees roberts
ELAPHITI ISLANDS, CROATIA

I will never do a renovation in Croatia again," vowed Lucien Rees Roberts after a disastrous client experience on a tiny island off the coast of Dubrovnik. But just two months later, after a string of well-timed coincidences gradually changed their opinion of the area, he and his business and life partner, architect Steven Harris, began creating Villa San Spirito, the getaway home they now visit every chance they get. Recalling that period, Rees Roberts says, "It began with an email announcing that a fifteenth-century house was suddenly for sale, then another saying a house from the same era and on the adjoining lot was on the market. We went for an interview to prove the worthiness of our design intentions and that was it: five acres with four buildings we could transform into a main house, guest house, guest cottage, and painting studio, each with amazing views."

It was not easy—the contractor quit, everything had to be imported, and the resident donkey refused to transport the construction materials from the bay to the house at the top of a narrow, 156-step incline. The island, which remains nameless to guard the privacy of its 140 residents, is, in the designer's words, "Magical, tranquil, with the chug of boats barely audible in the distance, no cars allowed, and the most beautiful light."

Starting with the main house, they put up a new but historically accurate tile roof, installed plumbing, and—most important for retaining the feel of the ancient past—removed the tar, cement, and pine paneling that shrouded the limestone walls. As for the décor, "I dreamt it," says Rees Roberts. "In my mind, I walked through the rooms, deciding what to get and where to put it."

The design was conceived to help them enjoy the age of the house. "Modern but not harsh, comfortable, and warm," Rees Roberts says. The rough walls in the living room surround a coffee table with a base of gnarled olive branches, an arched niche with a basin for dispensing water that is original to the house, and Jorge Zalszupin's circa 1959 rosewood-framed chairs from Brazil. The colors throughout are muted in deference to the stone and the ash flooring.

"It's truly a paradise," says Rees Roberts. "The best part might be our simple daily routines, from picking breakfast right out of our citrus grove to boating over to neighboring islands for dinner with friends. Thank goodness I gave the place a second chance."

BELOW *Off the painting studio, a shower incorporates rock original to the centuries-old structure and features a carved stone basin, previously a gutter on another house restored by the designer. Terra-cotta floor tiles in a weathered hue complete the rustic look.* **RIGHT** *Sheltered by an original wood-plank ceiling, the master bedroom contrasts smooth and rough, curved and straight. The vintage Lucite lamps* are by Dorothy Thorpe, the 1966 Ribbon Chair is by Pierre Paulin, and the bedside tables were constructed locally in a design that reveals the stone against which they rest. **PREVIOUS PAGES** *A local blacksmith directed by the designer fabricated the fireplace. The metal hood is painted metallic black, the base is concrete. A Jasper Morrison cork ottoman and rush chair from the 1960s sit in front.*

Saarinen chairs surround a cerused white oak table designed by Rees Roberts and accented with Dorothy Thorpe's midcentury candlesticks. Philip Shinnick's wood diptych provides decorative texture.

stephen shubel
LOIRE VALLEY, FRANCE

Francophile that I am," says Stephen Shubel, who normally resides in San Francisco, "I had often thought about a home in France. And where better than the Loire Valley?" So when antiques dealer Sophie Prételat, a neighbor of the friend he was visiting one summer, told him about a 400-year-old house in a tiny village in the Angers countryside a few kilometers away, he thought, *"Parfait!"*

"Living in such an old house in such an old village," Shubel says, "is like inhabiting another century. Plus, it was always my fantasy to decorate something really ancient. A stone's throw from the Eglise de la Paroisse de St-Pierre en Vallée, a frequent stop for tourists, Shubel's *petit maison* is part of a compound that was once a convent, and is connected to the church by a tunnel. While the tunnel is now blocked off, the adjacent cellar keeps wine at exactly the right temperature. Little was needed in the way of remodeling. Shubel built an entryway to the wisteria-laden garden, added shelves beneath the studio/guest room's peaked ceiling, and installed French doors to give the interiors more light and better views.

"I was like a kid in a candy store when the decorating began," the designer says, "buying like crazy at flea markets, antique shops, and *brocantes* in the region." He notes that *les puces* in Montsoreau and Chinon are two favorites. Using white as his primary color for its ability to make a space with many things look uncluttered and serene, he arranges old and new, funky and fine into charming scenarios. An Empire chair in the living room, for example, gets updated with hemp upholstery. Seating from British retail chain Habitat pulled up to the fireplace—often used on cold winter evenings—takes on an expensive air. His chicken-wire-windowed kitchen cabinet, made by the previous owner, hides Shubel's washer and dryer, along with old crockery. And the nineteenth-century, mahogany-framed porcelain bathtub bought from a nearby château conjures thoughts of simpler times.

Underscored by the structure's original stone and terra-cotta tiles, remnants of the house's original architecture—some dating back to the 1600s—and such furnishings as the bedroom's wall-length cabinet that came with the house establish a distinct ambience: past meets present with comfort and élan.

Shubel keeps himself busy by reinterpreting traditional French dishes with a Californian twist for friends, drinking in the culture—"Did you know you can bring mushrooms to the pharmacy and they'll tell you if they're edible?" he asks—scoping out new design sources, and hiking. If ever at loose ends he searches local bulletin boards and newspapers for *greniers vides*—empty attics. These are village markets where residents literally pile their secondhand wares out in the streets. Every week he finds at least three or four treasures nearby.

LEFT *Tangerine accents reminiscent of the flames that emanate from the nineteenth-century fireplace define the living room, including a floor lamp wearing a shade of wallpaper by Sophie Prételat, and velvet draperies. Earth tones from the room's original oak beams and artifacts that line the mantel provide contrast.* **PREVIOUS PAGES, RIGHT** *Centuries-old, thick walls are evident in a sunny bedroom corner completed with a nineteenth-century French daybed—actually an amalgam of many pieces. Its unusually small size makes it a perfect napping spot for Shubel's two papillons. The painted side table is 1940s Moroccan in origin, and was purchased at a Parisian puce.*

BELOW *Opposite the living room fireplace, a mirror purchased from a local dealer rests on an eighteenth-century fruitwood farmhouse table. The small, sloped door at floor level leads* *to the wine cellar.* **LEFT** *Under a peaked ceiling, beams embedded into a plaster wall create a free-form book-case.* **PREVIOUS PAGES** *Cabinets once prominent in an herbalist's shop now* *hold Shubel's collections of clock faces, artifacts, apothecary jars, and framed art. Eighteenth-century French prints and drawings hang on the wall.*

ronald bricke
PARIS, FRANCE

It all began with cooking classes at La Varenne. "A week in Paris and I was hooked," says Ronald Bricke. "I loved the city and everything about it. But living there? A pipe dream." One, however, that came true for the New York–based designer. Thanks to a friend of a friend, "a French Auntie Mame," he quips, he found the Place des Vosges *appartement* he's enjoyed for thirty years. Up three floors of a building once home to Victor Hugo, the 600-square-foot studio has a view of the courtyard below. When he bought it, there was nary a respectable closet in sight, but it had a fully-equipped kitchen and was in excellent condition. "I decided on it that very day," he says.

"I imagined exactly how I'd lay it out, from the furniture to the decorative elements and storage," Bricke recalls. "I just didn't have any pieces!" But before shopping, he created a serene "shell." The delicate color he chose for the walls that changes ever so perceptibly from morning to night is not a simple splash of paint. It's a faux-parchment finish created by friends from New York's Isabel O'Neil Studio Workshop, which he knew would enhance the delicate textures of the furnishings he envisioned. As the artists worked, Bricke oversaw two important installations: a washer-dryer and an eight-panel *paravent,* or screen, he designed that frames four 8-foot-high cupboards; the folding doors open to reveal built-in shelves. "It was a bit difficult explaining my drawing to the craftsmen," he recalls, "but the last thing I wanted was to take up space with closets." Utilitarian as well as decorative, the piece adds shape to the room and subtly reflects the angles in the parquet de Versailles floor.

Less successful was Bricke's original plan for eighteenth-century décor. Upon seeing the exorbitant prices, he decided that Art Deco pieces—much less expensive—could work equally well. Two weekends of storming Les Puces, the Porte de Clignancourt flea market, yielded almost everything he needed. Then magically the missing items began to appear; first an ottoman, next, two leather chairs identical in color to those he had in peach-hued velvet, and finally a secretary fronted with parchment that matched the walls. Visiting four or five times a year for ten days at a stretch, and always making a trip to the antique market, he has come to know many venues. Among his favorites on the rue des Rosiers are the Marché Biron and the sprawling Marché Serpette, which encompasses more than 150 vendors selling everything from rare *objets d'art* to 1960s furniture.

"I always imagined one of my favorite sculptures, the *Winged Victory of Samothrace,* was hovering over my shoulder," says Bricke, "opening doors to unique advantages, protecting me. Of course, the 1980s were the perfect moment to buy in Paris—with the dollar so strong, it fell into place easily. I'm a lucky man."

LEFT *A soaring glass Art Deco lamp wrapped in wrought iron joins a hammered-silver vase and 1950s pitcher on a small marble table designed by Bricke. Leather chairs were a lucky flea-market find— they are identical in color to chairs upholstered in velour Bricke already owned.* **BELOW** *A daybed stands next to a low marble coffee table; the room's paravent conceals shelving to keep the room visually uncluttered.* **PREVIOUS PAGES, RIGHT** *Nearly all furnishings in the studio, from the 1930s Art Deco chairs to the brass urn—originally one of a seven-piece garniture—on the parchment-fronted secrétaire are from Paris's Porte de Clignancourt flea market.*

william brockschmidt
MODICA, SICILY, ITALY

We owe Goethe great thanks for Casa Grotta, our house in Modica," says William Brockschmidt, only half joking. He had been reading *Italian Journey* and the line "To have seen Italy without having seen Sicily is to not have seen Italy at all, for Sicily is the clue to everything" hit a chord with him as he and his partner, architect Richard Dragisic, were planning a sabbatical from their demanding jobs. "So off we went to Sicily for a month. And we couldn't get enough of it—the people, food, wine."

A mere two visits later, the couple was convinced a house of their own was in order. Built into the side of a hill in Modica—a town they especially liked because "It's not a resort, it's urban like we are"—were two stucco houses, one atop the other, creating a potential for 1,800 square feet of total space. "All" they needed to do, says the designer in his self-effacing way, was to build a connecting interior staircase, remove decades of debris, reroute plumbing and electricity, and, because the town is a UNESCO World Heritage site, comply with dozens of regulations along the way. The huge, dirt-floored cave, to them, was added value. "They're very common here," explains Brockschmidt. "They've been used as barns and houses since six hundred B.C. And ours is dry, not damp as many are, so it wasn't much of a stretch to imagine it as a spectacular kitchen and dining area."

"My goal was to create a fresh take on Sicilian style," he says. "I wanted to particularly emphasize the contrast between the atmospheric cave downstairs and sunlit living room upstairs. I also used salvaged materials and local furnishings whenever possible." The vaulted "palazzo room," as they call the living room, features *cornici* he and Dragisic painted around the French doors—a modern version of Sicilian baroque ornamentation, which Brockschmidt explains, "can sometimes seem cartoon-y or naïve"—and a demilune, flip-top table from the early nineteenth century, frequently moved into the cave for dining. "Tiling all the floors, as was historically done, would have been outrageously expensive," Brockschmidt says, "and look too fussy for our modern tastes. Besides, we liked the rich hues of the native *pietra pece* stone that was already in place. So we have very little of it; just some historic remnants in the baths and in the living room, where we created a simplified rendition of a pattern we saw in a church in Ragusa, to add a formal note."

Pieces like the Louis XV–style chairs in the living room hail from flea markets, while such items as the circa-1800s *arte povera* entry table, painted to simulate marble on top and mahogany on the legs and apron, have antique-shop pedigrees. Two favorite haunts of Brockschmidt's are La Soffitta di Arena Marcella and Antichità Crisafi, both in Catania, an hour and a half away.

A few accessories made their way from other countries, such as bedspreads from New York—their hometown—the Moroccan lantern in the entry, and a Catalonian console in the bath. But the limestone cave? Purely Sicilian. What's more, "It's quite possible it was once an ancient tomb," says Brockschmidt. "But we've never had an uninvited ghost crash our cocktail parties!"

A Viennese lamp with a burnished metal base was chosen for its cartoonish shape that imitates the living room's handpainted blue cornici. The Louis XV–style chair, one of a pair found in a local flea market, upholstered in gauffraged velvet cut into the Louis Vuitton logo pattern, a Sicilian demilune table, and a leather-seated Biedermeier chair add more traditional touches.

LEFT *The pietra pece–floored loggia at the end of the hall was opened up by the designer during remodeling. The staircase connects two originally separate homes and directs light into a ground-floor cave. Wrought-iron railings bent to create the illusion of "nosing" at tread level appear particularly prominent against the plaster-over-stone walls. The pottery is from Caltagirone, known for its thousand-year-old craft tradition.*

BELOW *Monastic in its simplicity, the guest room is illuminated with natural light from the courtyard's arched doorway and oculus as well as a Kartel pendant light purchased in Messina.*

A limestone-walled cave, virtually untouched from its original condition, encompasses a sleek, contemporary kitchen that contrasts starkly with the rugged walls. Votive candles placed in existing niches and Moroccan lanterns add ambience.

lars bolander
VICKLEBY, SWEDEN

Settled by his Viking forebears in 8000 BC, Öland, a 4-mile-long, narrow island a few miles off Sweden's southeastern coast in the Baltic Sea, is Lars Bolander's home away from home. "I spent summers in Vickleby as a child," says the designer, who grew up in the nearby mainland city of Kalmar. "It's historic and beautiful," he adds, mentioning its ancient Roman village, bird sanctuary, and wild orchids found nowhere else in the world. "It's also in my blood." Bolander and his wife, Nadine Kalachnikoff, knew it was where they wanted to have a traditional, country-style getaway, but the few sites available—houses are usually passed down from one generation to the next—were underwhelming. Pressing forward, the couple turned to the Internet and chanced upon a 21-foot-wide, nineteenth-century farmhouse complete with a two-story, earth-floored barn a few feet away.

Upon seeing it, Bolander knew he would have to connect the buildings if they were to have sufficient living space. "How we were going to do this, I didn't know," he admits. "We just bought it and hoped for the best." The solution? Link them with an atrium. He removed the main house's sitting-room wall, added carved-wood columns from 1780 that he found at the Toulouse Antiques Fair in France to support the ceiling, and built steps of native *kalk* stone to access the barn, which is sited on lower ground. Then he installed a Juliet balcony with French doors on the top half of the barn wall and chiseled out a door on the bottom half to facilitate communication between all the connected structures. The main house now encompasses a sitting room, an expansive kitchen and dining room, two airy bedrooms, a bath, and a small office space. The barn comprises the master bedroom on the top floor and, below, an enormous bathroom with French doors that open to the garden.

Bolander mingles furnishings from Sweden, his former home in London, pieces picked up in Paris, his professional bases in Palm Beach and New York, and his worldwide travels. The décor, while light in color with pine flooring, very pale, glazed walls, and white-painted beamed ceilings, is not strictly Swedish. "It's more understated, with a spare aesthetic. I also added some neoclassical strokes with urns and busts," Bolander says. He even dresses some up with necklaces, just for fun. An abundance of paintings helps the space feel complete. Some, like Anthony Christian's, in the sea grass–floored sitting room, are contemporary, others, such as that of Queen Hedwig Eleonora in the atrium and the *dalmålning,* a tapestry-like painting of an old-fashioned Swedish wedding in the guest room, date from the eighteenth century. Bolander also uses frames in arresting fashion, as with the double-mounted portrait of a nobleman in the sitting room. As though this treatment might occur to anyone, he casually says, "I had two and they worked well together."

"Days go by quickly here," says Bolander. "Whether we're cooking, gardening, visiting friends, or traipsing through ruins, there's always something to do. And with the soft light bathing the island, it's extra appealing."

BELOW *Softly glazed walls, original beams, and a canvas-covered sofa provide serenity against a backdrop of eclectic art, which ranges from a portrait of a Swedish nobleman painted in the 1800s to a large 1970s piece by* British artist Anthony Christian. **LEFT** *Sea-grass floor covering anchors a sitting room that features a wax bust from early 1900s France, artichokes rendered by Henry Koehler, and a portrait of Picasso by Dalí atop* a Hector McDonnell pencil drawing. **PREVIOUS PAGES, RIGHT** *The entry is richly decorated: a red metal sconce from Palm Beach, wooden urns from London, a painted table from a Paris flea market, and a Swedish trunk.*

RIGHT *Trompe l'œil painted wood surrounds a tub in the master bath guarded by an antique bust purchased at Anthony Redmile Antiques in London. The tall cabinet is nineteenth-century Swedish. Radiant heating under the floors guarantees warm feet.* **BELOW** *Native kalk stones lead from an upstairs sitting room down to a 20-foot-high atrium and landing graced with a nineteenth-century French chair and pair of American iron pugs. Swedish King Carl XIV Johan gazes across the space from atop a wood column; a framed Scottish coat of arms and an English nobleman's portrait adorn the wall.*

An antique French, eighteenth-century cane chaise longue purchased in Stockholm is situated cozily in front of the master bedroom's plaster fireplace, original to the house. Glass-paned doors open onto an atrium that provides a direct view into the sitting room.

New beams hewn to appear old support the guest room's pitched roof, offering a simple counterpoint to ornate decorative touches including a bust adorned with necklaces, sweetly embroidered linens, and a tapestry-like painting.

URBAN
RETREATS

juan pablo molyneux
PARIS, FRANCE

I heard of a property you will love," said Juan Pablo Molyneux's assistant, speaking of a 1,000-square-foot residence within a sizable *hôtel particulier* built in 1619 that had been divided into eight separate dwellings. Intrigued, Molyneux rushed to the Marais to take a look. Its historically illustrious pedigree, a *cour d'honneur*, landscaped gardens, and the possibility of massive interior expansion if Molyneux bought neighboring apartments quickly convinced him to buy.

Although born in Chile, Molyneux's French roots date back hundreds of years. He and his wife, Pilar, had been looking for a Paris abode that was suitable for hosting numerous benefits. Like their New York townhouse, it also needed to serve as a base of operations as they shuttle around the world working on client projects.

Gutting the space brought ecstasy *and* agony. On the plus side, the process revealed the formal salon's original timber ceiling, a masterpiece that still retained the first owner's monogram incorporated into the painted design. On the minus side, Molyneux had to spend hours upon hours trying to obtain legal permission to build a staircase to unite the first and second floors in the several apartments he eventually purchased and joined; the French government has approval over structural changes in any *monument historique*.

The combined space is certainly grand. There are two of everything: living room, salon, and library. There is also a completely separate guest wing. The designer avows, "We use every inch." While the interiors are sumptuous in a way that suits the architecture, Molyneux explains, "As with all my work, I try to distill that which is expected into something unexpected." The elegant, Gustavian-influenced dining room is a prime example. Inspired by Christophe Huet's *Grande Singerie* at the Château de Chantilly, he had the walls hand-painted with frolicking monkeys—sometimes doing naughty things—a motif the couple decided to repeat on its custom-made Limoges tableware. Another instance of the designer's lighthearted spirit is the fourteenth-century limestone vault used as a wine cave and informal entertaining area. Here the designer placed cowhide-upholstered seating framed with rams' horns by Michel Haillard, which he dubs "Flintstone-esque."

Art is everywhere, and ranges in style from 1920s constructivist Aleksandr Rodchenko's wood composition in the entry hall to twentieth-century abstract works. A Turgot map of Paris, circa 1734, notably features the house. The furnishings can also be considered fine art: the scagliola-walled salon alone features an early-seventeenth-century commode bearing an early application of chinoiserie, one of three settees made by Georges Jacob for Marie Antoinette, and Diego Giacometti–designed coffee tables.

Perhaps the most spectacular part of the house is the entry vestibule. Depicting historic, now demolished, châteaux Marly and St. Cloud with 9,000 hand-painted tiles prepared by Atelier Prométhée, it took a full year to create and install. Molyneux says that Paris is "a master class for anyone in design." His home is, as well.

LEFT *Light pours into a salon through original leaded-glass windows curtained in silk. Accent pieces range from an eighteenth-century porphyry plaque depicting a Roman emperor high above a scagliola-framed door, to a lamp with a base made of a balustrade from post-Revolution Versailles, and a delicate painted table from eighteenth-century Italy.* **BELOW** *While Gustavian in overall appearance, most of the furnishings in the hand-painted dining room—besides the chairs—are not actually Swedish. The chandelier was designed by Henry Delisle for Grand Duke Paul, son of Catherine the Great, and the table is eighteenth-century Georges Jacob.*

Light from this chandelier once brightened an ancient Russian basilica. The 10-foot-long bench is by William Kent and references the gardens of Liancourt, represented in the azulejo-style wall tiles, each of which was numbered to ensure correct placement during the room's installation.

BELOW *The house's cave measures 30 by 40 feet and can seat twenty-four for dinner. The gilt-wood sconces take inspiration from Louis XIV, and the Provençal-style oak table that dates to the 1600s is decorated with pottery purchased in San Gimignano. Swiss cow bells embellish the hide-and-horn seating arrangement.* **RIGHT** *Furnishings from many countries unite in a home office. A statue of Antinous depicted as Osiris presides over the office while Russian mahogany chairs rest beneath tall windows, an Italian nineteenth-century chair sits to the side of the desk, and a seventeenth-century Dutch chandelier casts light on the grouping.*

Intricate detailing on an eighteenth-century rug from Agra pairs well with equally ornate, original, painted beams and begins a theme of decadent textiles that continues throughout the salon. The long, narrow tapestry between the windows is Louis XIV–era, the small piece above the wooden door panels is sixteenth-century Flemish, and the large one to its right, entitled "Diane Entre les Géants," dates to the early seventeenth century. The pair of upholstered chairs are circa 1720, and the tall bronze lamps set on Louis XV tables to either side of the Molyneux Studio sofa are English, circa 1850.

BELOW *Inspired by Paris's renowned Le Meurice hotel, a marble-and-tile guest bath sparkles in contemporary glory.* **RIGHT** *Contrasting textures add visual interest to a guest room. The hard surface of the birch-and-oak patterned floor is tempered by silk damask on the walls and the four-poster bed frame is wrapped in silk velvet. A commode accented by two eighteenth-century Chinese papier-mâché figures and a seventeenth-century engraving by Charles Le Brun portraying Alexander the Great in battle complete the space.*

alessandra branca
ROME, ITALY

Rome is my compass. It makes me stay true to who I am," says Alessandra Branca, whose second residence is in a former monastery in the Campo de' Fiori, the very neighborhood in which she was raised. The building is a rarity for its fifteenth-century facade but modernized infrastructure. "We didn't have to do anything but paint."

Although she adopted Chicago as her home in the 1980s, Branca still loves visiting her family and friends in Rome, where life happens more spontaneously. It's also convenient for business. "I can hop a plane or train to clients in neighboring countries and be back in time for dinner with Mum," she asserts. Indeed, she credits her mother for the warm hues of her apartment walls. "I wanted to celebrate Rome's light," says Branca, "but no one Pantone chip did it justice. So my mother, an acclaimed artist, taught me how to mix paint colors—just as they did five hundred years ago." Once that was finished, she began assembling furnishings, finding them primarily in the city. The designer says, "Superb antiques like those at Antichità Alberto Di Castro, gorgeous fabrics, and unique pieces made by master craftsmen are easy to track down. But a toaster? Extension cords? I had to bring them from home."

Branca's philosophy of living simply but well permeates her three-bedroom apartment, beginning in the entryway. She believes that multiuse spaces have more character than single-purpose rooms, so rather than a foyer, the front door opens into a spacious room that functions as den, office, and second dining area. The refectory table, similar to one the priests who lived here two centuries ago might have used, expands for meals and work; leather-upholstered chairs from the 1830s can be moved about as guests come and go; and the *secrétaire* with trompe l'œil antiquarian editions features a hidden drop-front desk that's as convenient for serving drinks as sketching.

Graphic colors and textures, particularly a fresco by seventeenth-century Flemish artist Paul Brill that Branca rescued from a palazzo about to be demolished and striped draperies, evocative of the uniforms worn by the Vatican City's Swiss Guards, add visual zing. In the breakfast nook, she mixes art with Indian-patterned pillows and a French tablecloth. The master bedroom's mood, however, differs dramatically from the rest of the apartment. A serene mossy green, elegant in its simplicity, it is like the one she has in the States.

"Being there, visiting museums, going to the market, doing normal, everyday things gives my work depth," Branca says, "and, I think, makes it better."

BELOW *Ticking on a nineteenth-century recliner and original leather on a masterfully carved side chair from the 1830s contrast subtly with the more modern treatment of a black leather–edged parchment shade on a lamp.*

A small collection of natural objects housed in glass bell jars adorn the top of a secrétaire. **LEFT** *Pompeiian-inspired paintings and frescoes by Branca's mother dictate the breakfast nook's color palette. Folding chairs*

allow for quick and easy seating adjustments when visitors arrive. **PREVIOUS PAGES, RIGHT** *The entry is floored in reclaimed terra-cotta tiles and anchored by a refectory table.*

RIGHT *Simple curtains of wool-and-silk ticking, a contemporary lit à la polonaise, and a canvas-upholstered Louis XVI love seat create a mood of elegant simplicity in the master bedroom. The paint-on-board panels and frames are the work of Branca's mother.*
BELOW *Marble feet reproduced from Roman statues and mounted on terra cotta tiles dating to 100 AD represent members of Branca's family—her husband, three children, and herself.*
PREVIOUS PAGES *The living room sets deep red against patterns, which means easy maintenance—ideal for visiting grandchildren. An Indian rug bought in Rome, a cotton-striped ottoman, and paisley fabrics on both the corner table and Louis XV fauteuils disguise any signs of use.*

mica ertegun
BODRUM, TURKEY

I really don't know what possessed us to buy the *konak*," says Mica Ertegun with a laugh, speaking of her villa in ancient Bodrum, a port city three hundred miles south of Istanbul. When she and her Turkish-born husband, the late Atlantic Records cofounder Ahmet Ertegun, first saw the house in the early 1970s, she remembers that "It was completely dilapidated, a ruin. Women were washing their sheep in the yard." But something besides the waterfront location—maybe the gracefully arched front door or the muezzin's melodic calls to prayer from the neighboring mosque—caused the New York–based designer to stop a bicyclist and ask if it was for sale. The answer was yes.

The existing hundred-year-old structure was basically four walls, a roof, and a lot of rubble; it even included some scattered statuary fragments that may have rolled down from the circa-350 BC Mausoleum of Halicarnassus on the hill just behind it. They added fireplaces and amended the original floor plan to include two buildings that now enclose a study, staff quarters, laundry, and additional bedrooms—some with two bathrooms because "Couples shouldn't have to share."

"I wanted the décor to be completely Turkish," says Ertegun, "with the proportions of the past, but made for living today. Not too much furniture, and whitewashed for a cool feeling." Open spaces furnished in an Old World style feature large pillows on the floor. Utilizing the outdoors was also important to her; floor-to-ceiling shutters swing wide open onto a garden terrace, welcoming in refreshing breezes and offering views of apple, peach, and palm trees at one end and the sea at the other.

Ertegun combed Istanbul's Grand Bazaar and Bodrum's own market for native textiles, furniture, and ceramic tiles, and she bought carpets from Galerie Anatolia, a well-known shop in town. Some pieces, like the Eastern-inspired, contemporary chairs in the living room, she bought as-is. Others, like the table piled with books in the same room, are custom-made—as with the game table designed for trictrac, a form of backgammon. Gesturing to the lace-trimmed shades in the so-called "pasha's bedroom," for the nineteenth-century portrait hanging there, she says, "Turks are nimble-fingered when it comes to anything handmade and have a great eye for color."

"We spend the day outside, swimming, admiring the surroundings, and thinking of the history of this place . . . relaxing." Regardless of how many guests there might be, Ertegun has thought of every comfort, so visits here are nothing but tranquil.

LEFT *Mixing East and West, European plates mass around an antique French mirror on a classically whitewashed dining room wall. A head of a Roman soldier found in the garden anchors the custom-made table and sits between wooden candlesticks and ancient pots from Israel. Two sefertasi, traditional Turkish lunch pails, rest next to the table's legs.* **PREVIOUS PAGES, RIGHT** *Referencing the tents of ancient Turkish peoples, a length of canvas floats over an outdoor dining area. The table, wood-and-rush chairs, and place settings are all local finds.*

RIGHT *Watched over by an Ottoman official, nearly everything in the stone-walled "pasha's bedroom" hails from Istanbul's Grand Bazaar, including the brass bed and the quilted-cotton table covering. The curtains, however, were made by local seamstresses.*
PREVIOUS PAGES *Framed examples of calligraphy decorate the living room. Turkish fabrics cover the sofa pillows and chairs, purchased at the Grand Bazaar. The room's upper shutters open outward and the lower open vertically; both reveal a garden view.*

thomas bartlett
LA PEÑITA DE JALTEMBA, NAYARIT, MEXICO

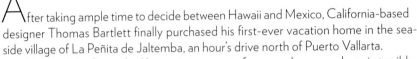

After taking ample time to decide between Hawaii and Mexico, California-based designer Thomas Bartlett finally purchased his first-ever vacation home in the seaside village of La Peñita de Jaltemba, an hour's drive north of Puerto Vallarta.

Hacienda La Peñita had been sitting empty for several years and was in terrible condition. Directing renovation via email, phone, and fax from his Napa headquarters, Bartlett transformed walls into French doors, replaced mildewed ceiling beams, and pushed out the walls of several rooms to add space. Within nine months, the red-tile-roofed, white-stucco house was ready for him and his continuous flow of guests.

The mélange of styles in the master bedroom is signature Bartlett. "I strive for a mix of furnishings that flows together," he proclaims. Here he combines regal nineteenth-century Portuguese chairs, an Italianate headboard depicting mermen wrestling with dolphins—he dreamt up the motif—and a traditional Mexican lantern of German silver.

The *equipal* chairs and stools—crafted by stretching leather over wood—in nearly every room are authentic, but custom built to be larger than most. As Bartlett explains, "My six-foot-four-inch frame tends to overpower smaller-scaled, ready-made versions." Artwork gets his personal stamp, too. One favorite is the custom-ordered floor-to-ceiling embroidered wall hanging in the dining area; executed by Puerto Vallarta's Villa Maria Decoración, it is not only beautiful, it serves the function of hiding a window that disrupted his design scheme.

Rugs from Oaxaca, India, and France, intricately painted furniture and lavishly patterned *talavera* pottery—made continuously in Mexico since the sixteenth century—are the favored accessories to complete the estate's look. While he admits many museums would relish acquiring some of his possessions, Bartlett is also no snob. He points out luncheon flatware purchased at a Cost Plus closeout sale as proof. "If it works," he says, "it's OK by me."

Bartlett's knowledge of the area is encyclopedic, thanks to visits about every six weeks . . . that sometimes last three weeks. He has immersed himself in its history, and eagerly tracks down the best resources for home goods. Hand-blown two-dollar glasses? "Try the factory retail outlets lining the highway between Tlaquepaque and Tonalá, a long drive, but chock-full of well-priced, good-looking items." One-of-a-kind ceramics? "Jesús Guerrero Santos is the best."

Life is *idílico* south of the border; though in daily touch with his office, Bartlett entrenches himself firmly in his adopted community. He is well-known in the neighborhood for participating in charitable endeavors with organizations like Women for Women and Los Amigos de Jaltemba—and for hosting margarita-laden extravaganzas.

LEFT *The master bedroom is carpeted with an Indian dhurrie and brightened by lamps shaded in leather-lashed vellum and lively artwork. The painting, by Katherine Ottesen, is entitled* Hotel Playa Puerto Vallarta; *the door, based on a sketch of Bartlett's, was executed by the muralist Antoinette Baronesse von Grone.* **BELOW** *Opening onto manicured lawns, the guest bath is highlighted by a vanity inspired by Portuguese tiles. The mirror, with an embellished, antiqued mirror inset frame, is from San Miguel de Allende.* **PREVIOUS PAGES, RIGHT** *A sturdy Mexican table over one hundred years old provides strong contrast to two ornate, eighteenth-century, silver leaf–embellished chairs from Mallorca. A chest from Galerías Arther in Guadalajara, topped with favorite pieces from the designer's talavera collection, and an enormous handcrafted, embroidered wall hanging typical of the region complete the vignette.*

RIGHT *Made for genial gatherings, the living room's canvas-covered equipal furniture is tailored to fit the designer's tall frame. A 5-foot-high Huichol yarn-on-beeswax artwork depicting the indigenous peoples' culture is displayed in a silver-gilt frame, and antique silver-and-glass lanterns by Santa Fe's Ford Ruthling grace either side. An eighteenth-century French chest and a French linen-and-cotton rug underfoot provide a subtle European note.*
BELOW *Boston ferns line a stairway that shows off a 2001 painting by local artist Valentino Mendez.*

juan montoya
BOGOTÁ, COLOMBIA

It's nothing at all like my New York apartment," says Juan Montoya of his pied-à-terre in Bogotá, where he was born. "I wanted it to be pure, authentic Colombian, with all the furnishings purchased in the country. At the same time, it needed to evoke a sense of intrigue, mystery, and Zen." A tall order, but one put into action beginning at the entryway, where a parcel gilt console from the seventeenth century greets visitors, its legs perched on lions' paws and its top laden with *curiosidades*. A right turn into the living room reveals a granite fireplace of his own design, with posts suggestive of ancient plinths; and the spacious bedroom features lambskin-padded closet doors reminiscent of shoji screens. Such brews of museum-quality treasures and humble, country pieces echo throughout—simplicity at its most engaging.

Montoya's visits focus on childhood friends and family, as well as creating short breathers from work. "From the moment the plane touches ground," he says, "it's special. Friends come over for lunch or cocktails, we have long dinners out. My partner, Urban Karlsson, enjoys it as much as I do." It's easy to see why. In addition to being surrounded by the Andes Mountains, their red-brick apartment is poised on the city's highest point, offering a seemingly endless view of the world below, especially from the best seat in the house—a neoclassical daybed in the living room facing a terrace garden encompassed by the delicate fragrance of lush vegetation.

It all started with a complete gutting of the 1,100-square-foot space. Then Montoya created an envelope of traditionally prepared white plaster ceilings and walls and grounded them with *flor morado* hardwoods. Finally the furnishings arrived, the myriad styles and eras represented "thanks to centuries of South Americans holidaying in Europe and, before them, the invading conquistadors," Montoya explains. The bedroom showcases a wool blanket inspired by the ponchos of the Chibchas, an indigenous people; there's a gilt-wood armchair from nineteenth-century France, regally wearing its original brocade shot through with gold near the dining area; and a sitting room, furnished in Victoriana, boasts a coffee table with a base made of legs from a centuries-old *santos* figure the designer found.

Montoya divulges the appeal he finds in the sculptural fragments of legs, hands, and even heads scattered about: "They're artful expressions of the anatomy." Pausing a beat, he adds, a twinkle in his eye, "And I do have a sense of the macabre." For more conventional pieces, the designer turns to antiquarians Camilo Alonso and Jaime Botero, and the stores Las Casas and Artesanías de Colombia, for exquisitely crafted furniture based on designs from years past.

A curator at heart, Montoya describes his aesthetic as "elegant and concise, underscored by clarity and bolstered with an ethnic feel." Displayed with the assurance that only one so well versed in his craft could command, everything from the unfilled picture frames, which, as he says, "are as important as paintings," to the sturdy Colonial chairs contribute to a home that, despite its splendor, is simplicity at its finest.

LEFT *Silk-embroidered Italian wool from Montoya's textile collection covers a dining table abloom with calla lilies. Other accents include two gilded, wooden fragments from an altar table that gleam above the fireplace mantel and a bronze sculpture fragment. Cashmere draperies cocoon the room from the city's noise and lights.* **BELOW** *Painted in the manner of Bartolomé Esteban Murillo, San Juan de Dios is framed in gold leaf to make it pop against a living room wall.* **PREVIOUS PAGES, RIGHT** *Influenced strongly by French neoclassicism, the linen-upholstered daybed is from Colombia and draped with an English, nineteenth-century paisley shawl. The silver South American pitcher is circa 1625.*

BELOW *Among the curiosidades on the dining table are a miniature, sterling-silver, sixteenth-century chair used to display santos figures in churches and locally acquired Lalique pieces. The elaborate gilded frame, deemed lovely enough to hang empty, dates from the 1600s.* **RIGHT** *Mounted gilt-wood fragments from an altar table and nineteenth-century English chairs upholstered in Italian cotton counter sleek closet doors in a dressing area.*

LEFT *Crisp in Frette linens and backed by a screen of woven flor morado, a bed cozies up to a small table topped by the feet of a centuries-old santos figure. Sliding glass doors draped in taffeta open directly onto a balcony garden.*
BELOW *Some of Montoya's favorite wood hands, circa-1600s santos figures, an alabaster taza, an eighteenth-century silver Peruvian frame, and a mounted fragment of a pre-Colombian sculpture accent an entry table.*

timothy corrigan
PARIS, FRANCE

Timothy Corrigan lived in Paris for seven years during the 1990s, while running the European division of a global advertising agency. At the same time, he began dabbling in interior design as a sideline. When he was relocated back to New York to head the company's international division, he found that he missed the City of Light. "I didn't want to have once lived there. I wanted to live there *now*," he remembers.

Following the mantra "Do what you love and the money will follow," Corrigan decided to design full time, opening an office in Los Angeles. Several years of hard work later, his European business had grown enough that a Paris office made sense. There, he quickly became known for infusing European elegance with Californian casualness. While happy in his rented apartment, he kept his radar up for purchasing opportunities. Most of the places he saw had been stripped of the graceful moldings and boiseries he loves, however. "Finally a broker showed me a classic apartment near L'Opéra that hadn't been touched in a hundred years," he relates. It needed refurbishing, but it was "quintessentially Parisian." As for the décor composed for it, he laughs: "I channeled Proust and added some La-Z-Boy."

The two-bedroom, two-bath floor-through with 17-foot-high ceilings includes a barely used kitchen. Although he works nearly round-the-clock—"When it's nine at night in Paris, it's only noon on the West Coast"—Corrigan still throws frequent dinner parties. "It's easy with all the prepared delicacies available here, plus I like to have an excuse to use the dining room." Atelier de Ricou painted the trompe l'œil sky on the oval-shaped room's ceiling and refinished all of the apartment's woodwork.

Living two blocks from the Drouot auction house is also every designer's dream. "They hold ten sales a day, so being able to rush over at the drop of a hat makes it much easier to find exactly the right pieces for clients," he says. He has also found pieces for himself, noting the dining room's Directoire *secrétaire* and living room's painting of a "smirking" Roman emperor. Proximity to London also pays off—it's where he acquired the seventeenth-century *verdure* Aubusson tapestry that hangs behind his bed. It covers two of the apartment's nineteen doors; others he conceals with grand-scale paintings by French artist Hubert Robert.

"An abundance of doors were typical of the Napoleon III period, because symmetry was of great importance," says Corrigan. "It was *comme il faut* for there to be doors on each side of the fireplace, and furniture was often placed in a room's center rather than against the walls."

The Porte de Clignancourt flea market is another favorite haunt. "You never know what you might see," he enthuses. Cases in point: the dining table, Victorian chairs, and guest room's bedside lamps—whose bases were once part of a balcony rail. Corrigan mixes French antiques with Italian art, Tabriz rugs snapped up in Amsterdam, where he claims to find the best prices, and comfy, overstuffed furniture made in London to fill out the remainder of the 1,300-square-foot residence.

"I'm so alive in Paris," he says. "All my senses are at work. I really do feel *bien dans ma peau.*"

La Prusse

LEFT *Hand-gilded boiserie and silk taffeta drapes catch the light from a crystal-and-bronze chandelier. A Tabriz carpet and travertine marble coffee table imported from Italy continue the room's theme of opulent materials. The mirror above the sofa conceals an oddly placed window that looked into the dining room next door.* **PREVIOUS PAGES, RIGHT** *A vivid tableau of French objets in continual flux catches the eye: a bust of Louis XV by neoclassical sculptor Jean-Baptiste Lemoyne looks over a Sèvres porcelain jardinière and an eighteenth-century Porcelaine de Paris biscuit potiche with ormolu mounts.*

BELOW *A glimpse into the dining room reveals richly ornamented walls and an eighteenth-century chair upholstered in embroidered needlepoint, found at auction in London.* **RIGHT** *Griotte marble makes up a fireplace mantel topped by an original pass-through-food warmer. Local markets, such as the Drouot auction house and the Porte de Clignancourt flea market yielded the room's other furnishings, including the fruitwood, Directoire secrétaire and Victorian dining chairs, respectively.*

LEFT *Framed Italian crests from the seventeenth century flank a mattress-ticking curtain cascading from a guest room bed's gilded baldachin; these establish a black, white, and red theme continued in the houndstooth-patterned wool drapes.* **BELOW** *A vanitas painting—a genre of still life—from the 1920s sits atop an inlaid fruit-wood chest from France's Restoration period. The bench is Napoleon III.*

Light hues mediate the formality of the master bedroom's damask and ornate moldings—a 20-foot-wide tapestry featuring a pastoral scene even helps it exude a bit of country. While a Louis XVI chest had to be purchased at Christie's and tucked into a corner to conceal what is actually an extraneous doorway into the living room, the carved gilt-wood mirror above the fireplace needed no sourcing—it is original to the Napoleon III–era apartment.

BELOW *A study of Hercules rests on a marble-topped Louis XVI commode.* **LEFT** *Nineteenth-century copies of busts of the sons of Trojan priest Laocoön are poised on the living room mantel, along with an 1843 architectural model of a staircase, and carved-wood flames from the seventeenth century, once used to support candles in candlesticks.*

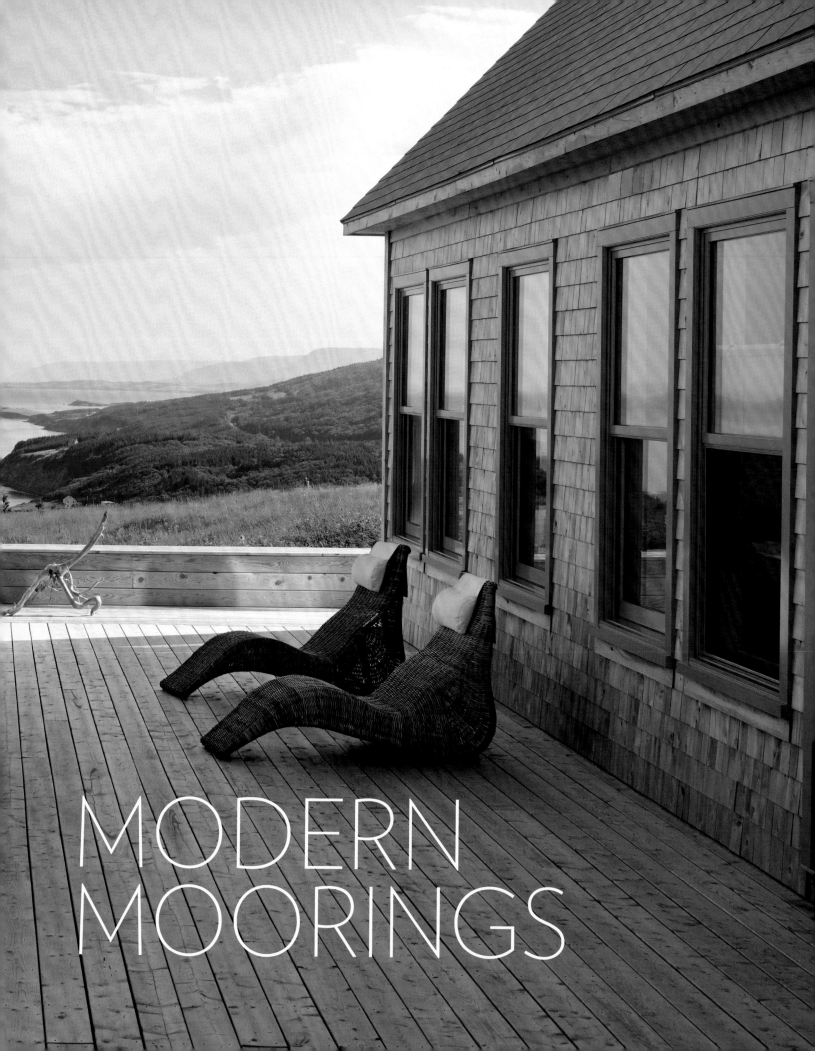

MODERN MOORINGS

alexandra angle
CAPE BRETON ISLAND, NOVA SCOTIA, CANADA

Composing a color palette is usually Alexandra Angle's first step when she designs an interior. For the vacation home she and her husband, Eliot, built on Cape Breton Island overlooking the Gulf of St. Lawrence and mountainous Highlands National Park, she says she was inspired by the landscape's "moody blues and grays, delicious greens and lavenders . . . completely different hues than those we have at home in Los Angeles."

Although the vacation house is the length of the continent away, she explains, "We're both from the East Coast and really weren't concerned about how often we might get there. We just thought it would be nice to have a house where our families could come in the summers or whenever our schedules permitted. We remind them that the water is warm enough for swimming!"

Angle purposely kept the cedar-shingled cottage's architecture simple so that it can withstand the freezing winters and periodic gale-force winds. She consequently doesn't worry about it sitting unattended for long periods. Built by local craftsmen mindful of the rugged area, the structure sports floor-to-ceiling windows facing every point on the compass and a wraparound deck of local pine.

"I wanted it to feel like a summer house," she says, "easy and relaxed, where sandy feet are OK and there's always room for unexpected items we might collect over the years." She succeeds with a mix of old and new, sleek and handcrafted pieces arranged in airy configurations.

A global roundup of furnishings, including many that reference the sea, holds court. Angle designed the slim birch table in the kitchen, flanked it with Giò Ponti's Superleggera chairs, and lit it with a chandelier from Turkey. "I cook a lot here—we never have time in L.A.—so it was important to me that the kitchen feels welcoming," says the designer. "But my truly favorite place is the colorfully cushioned window seat spanning the living room." The maple coffee table reminds Angle of the jellyfish—nonpoisonous—that surface once a year in the gulf, the rattan chairs, seashells, and the knitted-felt hassock, brain coral. "I don't like theme-y rooms," she says, "but I did want to project the idea of being near the sea. The need for some curves to counter all the straight lines was equally important."

Angle installs antiques and regionally crafted handiworks upstairs to homey yet clean-lined effect. Some, like the guest room's early-nineteenth-century sampler stitched by sailors to ward off boredom, are from Eliot's grandmother; others, such as the commode in the guest bath, rich with generations of flaking paint, are local finds. "We'd be kicking ourselves now if we hadn't listened to our contractor. Thankfully he suggested building guest quarters upstairs. We had been planning to use it as an attic."

LEFT *Eliot Angle crafted the master bedroom's plywood-topped side table from driftwood found in a stream leading to the nearby beach; Alexandra designed the rug, which a local artisans' cooperative wove. The beechwood* lamp is by Le Klint. **BELOW** *Serenely simple, a wood-paved master bath features an Angela Adams rug, a vintage tub found in Halifax, and antique stools picked up in Maine. The vanity is Alexandra's design.*

PREVIOUS PAGES, RIGHT *Paint on a vintage chair contrasts playfully with the modern finish of a Piet Boon desk made from corrugated cardboard. A felt light fixture by Mixko casts butterflies on the walls come night.*

Whale-watching can happen right from the living room, which reveals subtle sea shapes throughout. A custom Fedora Design rug is reminiscent of sprays of foam, shell-shaped rattan chairs are by Vittorio Bonacina, and a painted aluminum light fixture, called the "Octopus," from Autoban, hangs above.

LEFT *The functional space in the "living-room-dining-room-kitchen," as Alexandra calls the house's large, open area, is lined with beadboard cabinets and open maple shelving for the* cookware, china, and glasses she gathers on business trips. The rush-seated chairs at the table—which was built by a local craftsman—are Giò Ponti. **BELOW** *Thoughtful hosts, the* Angles provide appropriately themed bath-robes for their guests; they hang in a small guest room near an Alvar Aalto bureau, a gift from Eliot's grandmother.

fawn galli
COMILLAS, SPAIN

My husband, architect Julio Salcedo, grew up in Madrid," says Fawn Galli, "and Madrileños have a special affection for Comillas, a historic village in northern Spain on the Atlantic Ocean, for its mild climate, its welcome change from the city's dry heat, and its chic and understated atmosphere. It's all that and more for New Yorkers like us—a lovely place to retreat from our busy lives and for our two young sons to deepen their ties to the culture and our Spanish relatives."

The glass and *mármol Escobedo* stone structure that Salcedo designed for his family in the nearby countryside was "outside the vernacular of the contractor and team we hired from town," Galli says, "who are accustomed to building classical, red-tile-roofed homes. But I think they enjoyed the challenge of using stone from just two towns over in a nontraditional way."

Wanting the landscape of gently rolling hills to take precedence, Galli kept the interiors simple. Her key ingredients are bolts of strong colors against lots of white, and fluid shapes. "The hues I chose reflect what we see through the windows," she says. As for the furnishings, they were almost all sourced in Madrid. The designer spotted the guest room's Danish side chairs and retro, teak table at el Rastro, the capital's open-air flea market, and the living room's side table at Feriarte, the city's annual art and antiques fair. Even Zara Home was visited, which yielded festive dinnerware and bathroom accessories.

Perhaps Galli's favorite "shop," however, was her mother-in-law's closet. There she found handmade, delicately trimmed bed linens, candlesticks, flatware, and other Spanish heirlooms treasured by Salcedo's family that are an Old World complement to the contemporary house. Sculptures—a lacy, white wall piece by Alejandra Rein, an abstract on the terrace by Cándido Monge, and garden pieces by ceramicist Joan Llácer—reference the country's long artistic history in a way that creates a visual connection to her husband's heritage, and provides a more profound experience than simply visiting Spain.

Whimsical elements sprout here and there, reflecting the couple's playful personalities. The kitchen is set within a blue-green, freestanding box, its two entrances, one to the dining area, the other upstairs to the terrace, making it as practical as it is original. Galli hangs necklaces and bracelets on a chandelier in the guest room to pep it up, and she picked the tufted chairs and matching ottomans there and in the living room not only because they're comfy, but for their fun, big, black wheels.

"It's extraordinary how being in another country shifts your perceptions," Galli says. "I experience everything here from nature to architecture to daily realities with fresh insight. It's a good thing."

LEFT *A neutral walnut-and-stucco interior was chosen for its ability to accommodate frequent décor changes—a Sumak rug in winter is swapped for a cowhide in summer, for example, somber pillows for bright,* *and a low teak coffee table for a higher model.* **BELOW** *Local markets helped furnish the house; the 1940s leather-and-wood chair was found at a dealer in Madrid, and the vintage teak table, perhaps Danish in origin, was* *purchased at el Rastro.* **PREVIOUS PAGES, RIGHT** *Airy and light, Galli's living room is grounded by a Sumak from Istanbul's Grand Bazaar and a teak-and-glass coffee table from Las Molucas, a shop in Comillas.*

BELOW *A kitchen-in-a-box pops with lacquered color. Its walls conceal clutter, while strategically placed openings keep it in contact with adjacent rooms.* **RIGHT** *Bohemia comes to a sitting room lively with African fabric, a flea market chair and matching ottoman upholstered in linen, and a bejeweled Ikea chandelier. Salcedo's painting ties all the colors together.*

LEFT *The house's modern structure, designed by Galli's architect husband, reinterprets traditional vernacular forms.* **PREVIOUS PAGES** *Punctuated with doves by ceramista* Carmen Perujo *and a large, mythical piece constructed of iron, "El Grito del Fauno" by Cándido Monge bought at Art Madrid, the terrace is furnished with Ikea chairs and a custom, painted-wood table.*

sue firestone
THE TAMSEN

When Sue Firestone wants a change of scenery, she travels in style, taking family members and friends for an adventure on the *Tamsen,* her 171-foot yacht. Named for the family matriarch, the *Tamsen* travels the globe six months of the year, the designer on board for four of them. When she's landlocked, others in her "tribe" are often out riding the waves, pushing the boat's 14.5-knot maximum speed under full sail. But even when it's docked in Santa Barbara or Los Angeles, where she has her offices, the ship is still Firestone's favorite place to be. "We built it from scratch. It's our dream boat, our second home," she says.

Designed with a residential ambience, the vessel took premier Italian boating company Perini Navi two years to build. Indeed, it could easily be mistaken for a landlubber's palatial home, due in part to the abundant artwork, which includes a Joan Miró in the master stateroom and a selection from Firestone's favorite sculptor, Sergio Bustamante. Even the ship's most functional spaces receive careful attention: his-and-hers marble-clad "heads" feature stone she handpicked from four quarries in Italy, and the stainless-steel galley that would make any restaurant proud for its complete battery of professional equipment is positioned on the main deck, rather than below, which started a trend in yacht design. "I did it so everyone can participate," she says. "If I'm not chopping and sautéing, I can chat with those who are."

"On a boat," says Firestone, "you must maximize every inch. And since we usually have twenty to thirty people with us, including children, we definitely need all kinds of spaces." To combine good looks with inspired functionality the designer collaborated with the construction company's architect to create such wizardry as a bunk bed in one of the guest suites that disappears into the ceiling with the touch of a button, windows that electronically morph from clear to opaque to ensure privacy when the *Tamsen* is anchored in crowded ports like Portofino, Italy, and a "shell door" that runs parallel to the waterline to facilitate swift dives into the ocean.

It's so cozy, in fact, it's easy to forget it's a boat. A burled walnut table anchors the dining room, and is surrounded by chairs of Firestone's design that also flaunt upholstery fabric based on the family patriarch's art seen throughout. Set with Versace china and glassware, it's as elegant as the main salon, which is braced with super-soft Italian leather sofas that encircle marble-topped teak coffee tables. When night falls, the office desk in the master suite transforms into a vanity, and Firestone can slide beneath a silk bedspread and watch stars twinkling through the porthole. Would she ever live on it permanently? "Stranger things have happened," she says with a smile.

Open to a dinette area on one side
and an outside lounge area on the
other, the galley can also be closed off
with lateral, sliding doors. The counters
are finished in luxurious granite, and all
appliances are positioned for efficiency
of movement.

RIGHT *Firestone designed the teak-framed chairs in the salon and upholstered them in chenille to juxtapose with the kid-soft leather sofas and club chairs. The pillows' printed motifs are derived from Robert W. Firestone's art.* **BELOW** *A Jacuzzi on the fly bridge and plenty of seating on the main deck beg for crowds. Most of the seats, like the cushioned L-shaped benches, double as storage units for guests' belongings.* **OVERLEAF** *Cove lighting casts a romantic spell on the dining room in the evening. The ceramic piece on the windowsill is by Mexican artist Sergio Bustamante, and the decorative plate is Venetian glass.*

RIGHT *An interior envelope wrapped in teak and touches of walnut—on the bureaus' security railings and ceiling trim—is countered with tactile lush silk, velvet, and faux leopard. The coral-shaped lamps are polished brass.*
BELOW *In the bunk room, the bed at upper left folds up against the wall to create more headroom for the one below, and the bed at right rises into the ceiling at the touch of a button. The floor's wool carpet mimics the look of sisal, and hides a large storage area.*

clodagh
BALLINSPITTLE, IRELAND

"We wanted a property near the water that would be easy for the entire family—scattered about the world—to get to," says Clodagh. "I thought something that hadn't been a house might be interesting, and why not in my native Ireland?" Her sons started hunting and soon stumbled upon a possibility near Ballinspittle, on County Cork's southern coast, minutes from a beach where they could gallop horses, swim, and surf. Strewn with old-growth specimen trees, the four-acre meadow featured a 300-year-old stone building with views of the Atlantic Ocean and the Old Head of Kinsale Lighthouse.

The structure itself had been a cowshed; it was in a shambles and the roof had caved in. No matter. Clodagh flew in from New York, where her firm is located, saw its potential, and pronounced the 2,500-square-foot structure perfect for their needs. Eager to start, she assembled her children and their spouses to discuss renovations. "We're a creative bunch, and luckily share a similar aesthetic," she claims proudly. Listening as ideas bounced back and forth, she drew a plan. Everyone signed off on it and the work began.

After literally mucking out the building and excavating, Clodagh put on a new roof rigged with solar panels and skylights and fit the diversely shaped and sized windows with glass. She also installed radiant heating under newly poured concrete floors. This was not sheer indulgence—but it does make the floor feel like satin beneath bare feet—it keeps the house warm and dry, a must in the rainy climate.

"You needn't forego luxury to be 'green'," says the designer, who practices what she preaches by demonstrating her "life-enhancing," minimal style here. Art fills the residence—Coen de Beer's homage to Picasso above the fireplace, Jesús de Haro's 1975 painting in a bedroom, a piece by son Peter O'Kennedy in the dining area. A spa, complete with sauna and steam room, is another notable feature. Nonetheless, the kitchen maintains supremacy in terms of favorite gathering spots. "We're quite irascible about cooking," says the designer. To keep everyone happy she built an 18-foot-long-by-5-foot-deep concrete counter so eight people can work at once.

The few, yet exceedingly comfortable furnishings, she says, comprise "Everything we need, but nothing more than we need, and are built to last." Some, like the Squish sofas upholstered in outdoor fabric, benches, and communal table, are her design; others, such as the ceiling lights found in a junk shop in Amsterdam and a coffee table from Bali, for example, were lugged back by family members from their travels. Clodagh prefers Irish purveyors Wink for lighting fixtures and Thomas Ferguson for fine linens. "It feels like another world here. I come as often as I can, but it's never enough," Clodagh says.

LEFT *The one-of-a-kind cabinet behind the sofa is made from reclaimed wood and was designed by Clodagh's son Tim O'Kennedy, but built by Piet Hein Eek. A Connemara Mountains sheepskin edges the steel-faced fireplace, and the tall lamp in the corner, Clodagh's design, is made of stainless steel and acrylic shoji paper. The rug is from her Tufenkian collection.*
PREVIOUS PAGES, LEFT *Beams from an abandoned cotton mill in Georgia yielded a 16-foot-long table and benches; they were assembled before shipment to Ireland. The room's floor is poured and polished concrete. Behind the freestanding oak-veneered kitchen walls, a spa awaits.*

RIGHT *Guest bedroom walls of 300-year-old stones found on the site are enlivened by a photo taken by Clodagh, entitled* Montauk 2011. **PREVIOUS PAGES** *A bedroom decorated with old boat propellers—sometimes pressed into service as cheese boards—is lit by the very first lamp Clodagh designed, which came out in 1986.*

alison palevsky and sarah shetter
CABO SAN LUCAS, MEXICO

I was married—and honeymooned—on Mexico's East Cape, and absolutely loved it," says Alison Palevsky. "So when the time came to find a house for weekends and holidays, of course my husband and I thought to look there." Luckily they heard of a large, terraced residence perched on the edge of Cabo San Lucas; unluckily it needed a complete renovation. Not only was it embedded in huge boulders, the rocks peeked through the walls to the inside as well. But she and Alexander knew that even with the extensive work required to turn it into a sanctuary for family and friends, it was worth it. "You can't beat the one-hundred-and-eighty-degree view of Cabo's stone arches that mark the confluence of the Sea of Cortez and the Pacific Ocean," she says.

It was perfect timing for Palevsky to buy a house as well: she had recently established SPI Design in Santa Monica, California, with her friend, fellow designer Sarah Shetter, and the duo thought it would be a great project. "We went down for a week every month for a year to draw and plan," says Palevsky. "I don't think we could have achieved what we did if we hadn't had that on-site inspiration."

First came sandblasting. They ground down as many boulders in the 4,600-square-foot house as possible, and those that wouldn't budge were covered with concrete and plaster, then painted white. Floor-to-ceiling glass sliding doors were added and several rooms reconfigured to accommodate four bedrooms and bathrooms, media, dining, and living rooms, and a kitchen. On the lower deck they extracted several large rocks to enlarge the hot tub and pool, and on the upper patio they added a fire pit, bar, and *palapa*—a quintessentially Mexican, open-sided dining terrace with a palm-leaf roof.

The interior fittings were addressed last, with a goal of creating a pristine, light shell that maintained the integrity of the structure's Mexican roots. They lengthened the living room's built-in concrete sofa, laid cantera stone on the floors, and dressed up several bathrooms with Thassos marble. A light-and-dark theme works well to unify furniture originating from different eras and places. The dining room is furnished with Mexican, lattice-back leather chairs that encircle SPI Design's Tortuga table; the living room with a 1940s Warren Platner coffee table paired with African stools; and in the Ocean Suite—"We thought it'd be fun to name the bedrooms," says Shetter—the company's Cortez sofa faces a locally made rattan chair.

Two of Palevsky's favorite items are the "floating" bed she and Shetter designed and the master bath's three-ton tub, which had to be hoisted in through a skylight. *Definitivamente* there were challenges along the way. The biggest were the salty, humid air, hurricane season, and hefty taxes on shipments from the U.S. Making up for those, however, were the "exceptional" levels of craftsmanship they found in local carpenters and tile masons, and the wealth of stores in Todos Santos and San José del Cabo offering a broad assortment of handmade artwork, tableware, jewelry, and clothing. "Friends and family come thinking they'll spend their time sightseeing," says Palevsky. "But once here, they don't often leave the house."

LEFT *Matte steps of stucco provide a subtle contrast to the risers and make them easier to navigate; the railing was omitted to retain the stair's clean lines.* **BELOW** *Its sculptural form set into full relief against a white background,* a custom walnut table shows off iron candlesticks. The oversized wood vases hail from a Los Cabos shop. **PREVIOUS PAGES, RIGHT** *Floor-to-ceiling glass doors and windows abound, but the design team added a* skylight to increase illumination in the living room. The fireplace, with the exception of the new log-keep, is original to the house. As elsewhere, the floor is tiled in natural Rio Blanco cantera stone.

Designed for carefree living, the dining room chairs are cushioned in a durable Sunbrella fabric and the tabletop and Spanish-style serving niche are Corian. The iron chandelier comes from Tlaquepaque, an area famous for myriad lighting stores.

LEFT *The "Star Suite" is the most romantic bedroom in the house. Used simply but to dramatic effect, mosquito netting drapes a bed that appears to float, but actually rests on a massive* cement block concealed beneath its base. Rope supports lashed to white pine logs hand-sanded to a silky smoothness further the illusion. **BELOW** *Fitted with Dornbracht faucetry, a* travertine tub carved in France is big enough for two. The abstract wood sculpture, found in a Todos Santos gallery, is by an unknown artist.

BELOW *Shipshape to the utmost, every inch of the Ocean Suite, beginning with wood ceiling beams that conceal air vents, is used wisely. Sconces glow with an oil-rubbed, brass finish.*

RIGHT *Tropical touches, including a cooling rattan paddle fan and sisal flooring, tie the Ocean Suite's sitting room to its location. The chair is a Tlaquepaque find; the African table was shipped in from Los Angeles.*

Brazilian photographer Fernando Laszlo's Insect Series is a cheeky reference to the many exotic bugs the designers have encountered in Mexico. Sculpted walnut lamps, rattan ottomans, and a custom bolster enveloped in Cowtan & Tout raffia fabric add curves to the room's décor.

RIGHT *The palapa is a favorite place for lunch; a 10-foot-long mesquite table, out of the sun beneath palm leaves and surrounded by an amazing view, holds a crowd.* **BELOW** *The main terrace of Casa Tortuga—the house is named for a large tortoise-shaped boulder in front—reveals the view that convinced Palevsky to buy the property.*

ACKNOWLEDGMENTS

Writing a book is no small endeavor, especially coming directly on the heels of another, in this case, *Designers Here and There: Inside the City and Country Homes of America's Top Decorators*. But when one is surrounded by inspiring colleagues and supportive friends, not only is it possible, it is a gratifying experience.

Thus it was for *Designers Abroad*. My first and most heartfelt thanks go to the talented designers who allowed me into their private homes-away-from-home—I will be forever grateful for their genius in choosing such exciting locations. I was expecting France, Mexico, and Italy, but Sri Lanka? Thailand? South Africa? Croatia? Amazing!

I am also greatly indebted to Stacee Lawrence, my editor at The Monacelli Press, whose intelligence and insight is beyond measure; Andrea Monfried, for believing in the concept in the first place; Elizabeth White, for her commitment to reproducing the designers' work so accurately; Mikhaela Mahony, for helping me keep all the image submissions straight; Michelle Leong, for her beautiful layout; the designers and photographers, who contributed their envy-inducing images; and friends and family, who shared the experience with me, providing encouragement, advice, and when needed—enjoyable distractions.

PHOTOGRAPHY CREDITS

Lucas Allen: 172–73, 174, 175, 176, 177, 178–79, 180, 181
Diego Amaral: 152
Alexandre Bailhache: 160, 161, 162–63, 164, 165, 166, 167, 168–69, 170, 171
Woody Biggs: 84
Courtesy Alessandra Branca: 130
Boris Breuer: 210
Michael Calderwood: 22, 23, 24, 25, 26, 27
Grey Crawford: 36, 37, 38, 39, 40–41, 42–43, 44–45, 46, 47, 48–49
Valerie de la Dehesa: 183, 184, 185, 186, 187, 188–89, 190–91
Richard Dragisic: 7, 98, 99, 100–101, 102, 103, 104, 105
Ari Espay: 118
Marina Faust: 116–17, 119, 120, 121, 122–23, 124, 125, 126–27, 128, 129
Eva Finder: 106, 107, 108, 109, 110, 111, 112–13, 114–15
Scott Frances/OTTO: 74–75, 77, 78–79, 80, 81, 82–83
Tim Geaney: 10
Sasfi Hope-Ross: 203, 204–5, 206–7, 208–9
Michael L. Hill: 94, 95, 96, 97
Thibault Jeanson: 131, 132, 133, 134–5, 136, 137
David Kelly: 76
Eric Laignel: 202
Jonathan Lewis: 138, 139, 140–41, 142–43, 144–45
Gerry Mulford: 51, 52–53, 54, 55, 56, 57, 58–59, 60–61
Sioux Nesi: 182
Costas Picadas: 8–9, 11, 12–13, 14–15, 16–17, 18, 19, 20, 21
Tuca Reines: 153, 154, 155, 156, 157, 158, 159
Giuliano Sargentini & Emilio Bianchi: 193, 194–95, 196, 197, 198–99, 200, 201
Durston Saylor: 62, 63, 64, 65, 66–67, 68, 69, 70, 71, 72, 73
Brian Seitz: 192
Eduardo Solórzano: 146, 147, 148, 149, 150, 151
Tim Street-Porter: 2–3, 211, 212, 213, 214–15, 216, 217, 218, 219, 220–21, 222, 223
Gilles Trillard: 85, 86–87, 88, 89, 90–91, 92, 93
Courtesy Trisha Wilson: 50
Lasantha Wijeranthna: 28, 29, 30–31, 32, 33, 34, 35